AF489319

OLYMPIC SPORTS FOR KIDS: AMAZING SPORTS FOR CHILDREN OF ALL AGES

Speedy Publishing LLC
40 E. Main St. #1156
Newark, DE 19711
www.speedypublishing.com

Copyright 2018

All Rights reserved. No part of this book may be reproduced or used in any way or form or by any means whether electronic or mechanical, this means that you cannot record or photocopy any material ideas or tips that are provided in this book.

Sports help children develop physical skills, get exercise, make friends, have fun and improve self-esteem.

Basketball is one of the most popular sports in the world. Some of the worlds greatest athletes are basketball players.

Sprints are short running races in athletics. The most common distances are 60 meters, 100 meters, 200 meters and 400 meters.

Long jump is a track and field event. It is an attempt to leap as far as possible from a take off point. The athlete runs down the runway to the jumping pit which is made of sand.

Badminton
is a sport
played with
racquets and
a shuttlecock.
Players use
racquets to hit
a shuttlecock
over a net.

Gymnastics
is a sport
involving the
performance
of exercises
requiring
flexibility,
balance and
control.
Gymnastics
is one of
the world's
oldest sports.

Taekwondo is a Korean martial art with a heavy emphasis on kicks. Taekwondo is used for more than sport; it is also a form of exercise and weaponless self-defense.

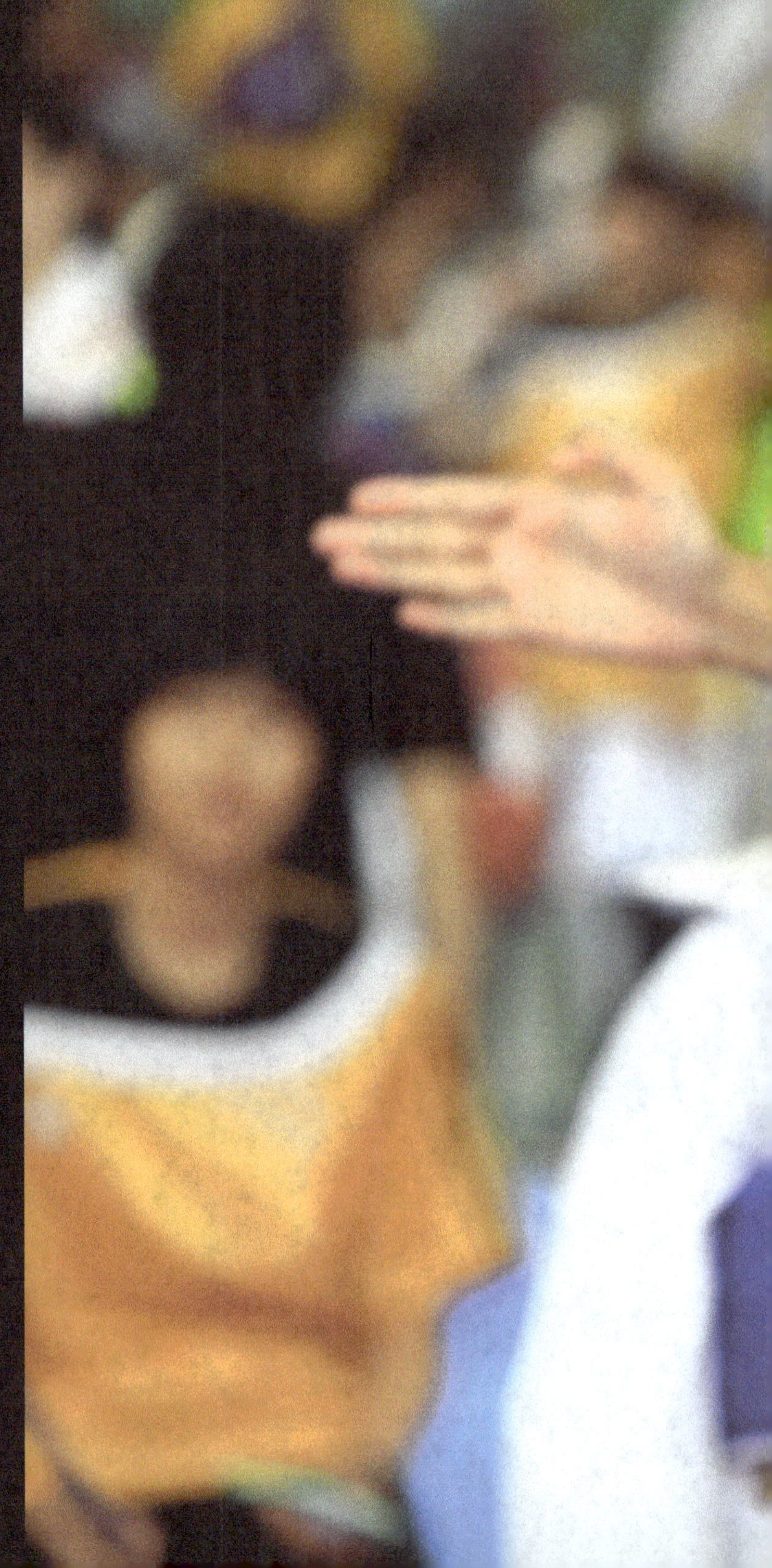

TAE   NDO

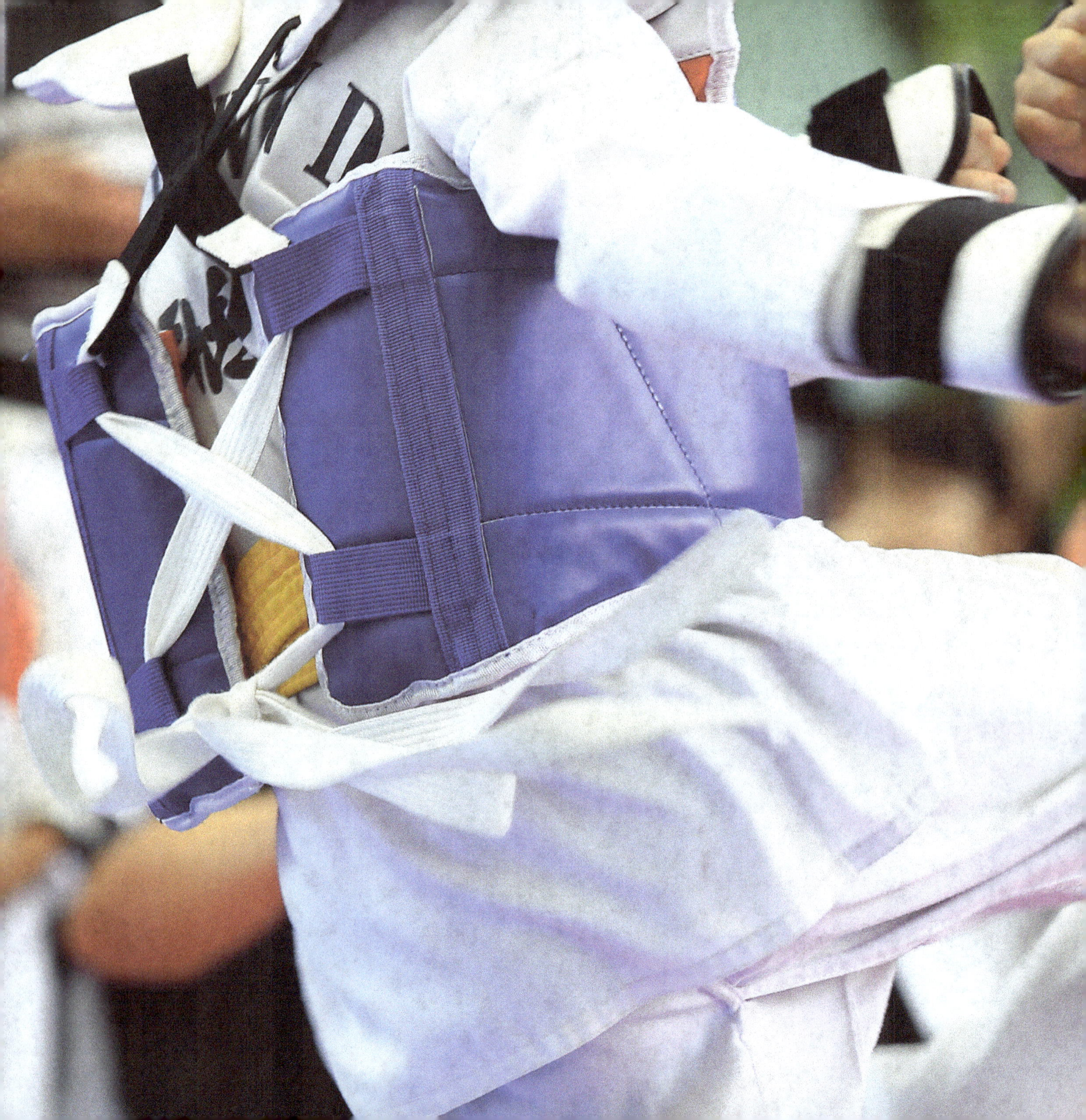

Swimming is one of the most popular Olympic sports. The four main strokes in swimming are, Butterfly, Backstroke, Breaststroke and Freestyle.

www.ingramcontent.com/pod-product-compliance
Lightning Source LLC
Chambersburg PA
CBHW080945130726
48003CB00010BA/3112